The
Fictionary
Dictionary

By Jim Marbles

The Fictionary Dictionary
ISBN 1-57757-019-7
Copyright ©1997 by Jim Marbles
P.O. Box 552
Jenks, OK 74037

Published by Trade Life Books
P.O. Box 55325
Tulsa, OK 74155

Introduction

Jim Marbles is a leading expert on little known facts and *misinforma-tion!* During his many years of research in the field of word origins, he has found "lost" definitions to many of our most commonly used words.

In this book you will find definitions that Noah Webster would never have included in his famous *The Webster's Dictionary*. If you have ever wanted to know the "unauthorized" meaning of words such as *Diagnostic or Kindred,* look no further.

The Fictionary Dictionary will entertain your intellect and tickle your funny bone. After reading this book you will no longer view words in the same light and may find yourself searching for "lost" interpretations of your own.

A la mode \a–le'–mod'\: served with
ice cream

Alarms \a'–larms\:
An octopus

Alarmist \a–lar'–mist\: a person who
tends to raise alarms

Ant \ant'\: any of numerous hymenopterous insects

Antacid \ant–as'–id\:
Uncle Acid's wife

Antagonism \an–tag´–u–niz–um\ :
active hostility or opposition

6

Antediluvian \an'-ti-du-loo'-vee-un\:
harking back to an earlier time

Antelope \an'-tl-op\:
How she married
my Uncle

Ante Meridiem \an'-ti-mu-rid'-ee-um\:
the period from midnight to noon

7

Antiballistic \an'–ti–bu–lis'–tik\:
designed to destroy missiles

Antibodies \an'–ti–bod'–es\:
Skeletal remains after you
bug spray the kitchen

Antibiotic \an'–ti–by–ot'–ik\: chemical
substances used to treat infectious

Arbitrate \ar'–bi–trat\: to determine

Arbitrator \ar'–bi–tra'–ter\:
A cook that leaves Arby's to
work at McDonald's

Arbor \ar–bur\: a leafy, shady recess
formed by tree branches

9

Architrave \ar'-ki-trav\: a molded or decorated band framing an opening

Archives \ar'-kivs\: What Noah kept the bees in

Archivist \ar'-ki-vist\: a person who collects or is responsible for archives

Avoid \a-void'\: to keep away from;
keep clear of; shun

Avoidable \a-void'-a-ble\:
What a bullfighter tries
to do

Avouch \a-vouch \: declare or assert
with positiveness

11

Balmy \bah'–mee\: mild and refreshing;
soft; soothing

Baloney \ba–lo'–ne\:
Where some hemlines fall

Balsa \bol'–suh\: a tropical American
tree yielding a light wood

12

Banns \banz\: notice of an intended marriage

Banquet \bang'–kwit\: Why the vocalist had no instrumentalists

Banquette \bang'–ket\: a long bench with an upholstered seat

Barrette \bu–ret'\: a clasp for holding a woman's or girl's hair in place

 **Barricade** \bar'–i–kad\: Where a grizzly plays video games

Barrier \bar–ee'–ur\: a limit or boundary of any kind

Berme \burm\: a mound of snow or dirt

Bernadette \burn'–a–det\:
The act of torching a
mortgage

Berry \ber–ee\: any small stoneless
juicy fruit

Boom \boom\: a deep, prolonged, resonant sound

 **Boomerang** \boo'–me–rang\: What's on top of a Ghost Cream Pie

Boon \boon\: something to be thankful for; blessing; benefit

16

Bottleneck \bot'-l-nek'\: a narrow entrance or passageway

Bottom \bot'-em\: What the shopper did when she found the shoes that she wanted

Bottomland \bot'-um-land'\: rich land which is especially good for farming

17

Boy \boi\: a male child, from birth to
full growth

Boycott \boi'–kot\:
What your son sleeps on
in camp

Boyfriend \boi'–frend\: a frequent or
favorite male companion; beau

Buckskin \buk'-skin\: a strong, soft, yellowish or grayish leather

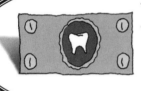

Bucktooth \buk'-tooth\: The going rate for the tooth fairy

Buckwheat \buk'-hweet\: flour made by grinding buckwheat seeds

Burglar \bur'-glur\: a person who commits burglary.

Burglarize \bur'-gler-ise\:
What a crook sees with

Burgle \bur'-gul\: informal, to burglarize

Caldron \kol'–drun\: also caul·dron, a
large kettle or boiler

Calendar \kal'–en–der\:
Someone who rents out
livestock

Calender \kal'–un–dur\: a machine for
impregnating fabric with rubber

Camp \kamp\: a place where a group
of persons is lodged in tents

Campaign \kam-pan'\:
Discomfort suffered
at a summer retreat

Campanile \kam-pa-nee-lee\: a
bell tower, especially one freestanding

22

Cannery \kan'–u–ree\: a factory
where foodstuffs are canned

Cannibal \kan'–e–bul\:
A potted meat product

Cannibalize \kan'–u–bu–liz\: to eat
human flesh

Cantabile \kan–ta'–bi–lay'\: songlike
and flowing in style

Cantaloupe \kan'–tl–op\:
When you are unable to
run away to get married

Cantankerous \kan'–tang–kur–us\:
quarrelsome; irritable

Cartoon \kar-toon'\: a drawing
symbolizing some subject or person

 **Cartoonist** \kar-toon'-ist\:
What you call your auto
mechanic

Cartridge \kar-trij\: any small
container for powder, liquid, or gas

Cast \kast\: to throw or hurl; fling

Castanet \kas'-te-net\: What they did to fill the role of Frankie Avalon's movie girlfriend

Castaway \kast'-a-way\: a shipwrecked person

Celt \kelt\: a prehistoric ax of stone or
metal without perforations or grooves

Celtics \sel'–tiks\:
What a parasite salesman
does

Cembalo \chem–bu–lo\: a keyboard
instrument, precursor of the piano

Commodity \ku–mod'–i–tee\:
something of use, advantage, or value

Commodore \kom'–e–dor\:
The entry to the bathroom

Common \kom'–un\: widespread;
general; universal

Concerning \kun–sur'–ning\: relating to; regarding; about.

 Concert \kon'–surt\: A breath mint for inmates

Concerted \kun–sur'–tid\: performed together or in cooperation

Consignment \kun-sin'-munt\: a
transfer to another's custody or charge

Consist \kon-sist'\:
A growth on an inmate

Consistency \kun-sis-tun-see\:
steadfast adherence to the same principles

Contend \kun–tend'\: to strive in debate; dispute

 **Content** \kon'–tent\: A fabric shelter for inmates

Contented \kun–ten–tid\: satisfied; content

Contrived \kun-trivd'\: obviously
planned or forced; artificial; strained

 **Control** \kon-trol'\:
A short, ugly inmate

Controller \kun-tro'-lur\: an officer
who superintends financial accounts

Convenient \kun–veen'–yunt\: at hand; easily accessible

 **Convent** \kon'–vent\: How inmates get air conditioning

Conventicle \kun–ven–ti–kul\: a secret or unauthorized meeting

Counterespionage \koun'-tur-es'-pee-u-nazh'\: the detection...enemy espionage

Counterfeiters

\koun'-ter-fit'-ers\: Workers who put together kitchen cabinets

Counterinsurgency \koun-tur-in-sur'-jun-see\: combating guerrilla warfare

Crest \krest\: the highest point or level; summit

Crestfallen \krest'-fo-len\: Dropped toothpaste

Cretaceous \kri-tay-shus\: resembling or containing chalk

Cross-examine \kros'-ig-zam-in\:
to question closely or minutely

Cross-eyed Teacher
\kros'-ied te'-cher\: A teacher
that loses control over his
or her pupils

Crossfire \kros'-fie\: when the lines
of gunfire cross one another

Derrick \der'–ik\: the towerlike frame work over an oil well

Derriere \der'–ee–aer\: The scent of being downwind of cows

Derring-do \der'–ing–doo\: daring deeds; heroic daring

Decoy \dee-koi'\: anything used as a lure

Decrease \dee-krees'\:
De fold in de pants

Decree \di-kree\: a judicial decision or order

Demoralize \di–mor'–u–lize'\: destroy the morale of

Demote \dee–mot'\: What de King put around de castle

Demotic \di–mot'–ik\: the current, ordinary, everyday form of a language

Despicable \des'-pi-ku-bul\: deserving
to be despised; contemptible

Despise \dee-spiz'\:
De persons who work
for the C. I. A.

Despite \di-spite\: contemptuous
treatment; insult

Détente \day-tont'\: a relaxing of
tension, especially between nations

 **Detention** \dee-ten'-shen\:
What causes de stress

Deter \di-tur\: to discourage or restrain
from acting or proceeding

Diagnosis \dy–ug–no'–sis\: an analysis
of the cause or nature of a problem

Diagnostic \di'–eg–no'–stik\:
A funeral of someone all dressed
up with nowhere to go

Diagonal \dy–ag–'–nul\: slanting;
sloping lines, ridges, or markings

42

Dictate \dik'-tat\: an authoritative order or command

Dictator \dik'-ta-ter\: Another name for Richard Spud

Dictatorial \dik'-ta-tor-ee-ul\: overbearing

Dilatation \dil'-u-tay'-shun\: an
abnormal enlargement

 **Dilate** \di-lat'\:
When a person lives longer

Dilatory \dil'-u-tor'-ee\: to delay or
procrastinate

Dioxide \dy-ok'-side\: an oxide
containing two atoms of oxygen

 **Dioxin** \di-ok'-sin\:
What you say before you kill a
herd of buffalo-like cattle

Dip \dip\: to plunge into a liquid and
emerge quickly

Distress \di–stres'\: acute anxiety, pain, or sorrow

 **Distressing** \di–stres'–ing\: What you put inside dis turkey

Distribute \di–strib–yoot\: distress or uneasiness of mind

Do-it-yourself \doo-it-yur-self'\: for
use by amateurs without special training

Doldrums \dol'-drumz\:

Percussion instruments played by
the Presidential Candidate
from Kansas

Dole \dole\: an allotment

Dreadful \dred'–ful\: extremely bad, unpleasant, or ugly

Dreadlock \dred'–lok\: The fear of opening the deadbolt

Dreadnought \dred'–not\: battleship with heavy-caliber guns

Eclectic \ee–klek'–tik\: not following any
one system

Eclipse \i-klips'\:

What a barber does
for a living

Ecliptic \ee–klip'–tik\: the annual path
of the sun in the heavens

Efficient \ef-fish-ent\: the least waste of time and effort.

Efficient \i-fish'-ent\:  The aroma from the seafood counter

Effloresce \ef-la-'res\: to burst into bloom; blossom

Efficacious \ef'–i–kay–shus\: effective as a means, measure, or remedy

 **Effigy** \ef'–e–jee\:
The letters between
E and H

Effigy \ef'–u–jee\: a representation or image

Elitism \i-lee'-tiz-um\: allegiance to a
select group

Elixir \i-lik'-sur\:
What a dog does to his owner
when she gives him a bone

Elizabethan \ee-liz'-u-bee'-thun\:
pertaining to the reign of Elizabeth I

 **Eucalyptus** \yoo–ke–lip'–tus\:
What the poodles said to
the groomer

53

Eustachian Tube \yoo–stay'–shun toob\: a canal extending from the middle ear to...

Euthanasia

\yoo–thu–in–a'–zha\:Young people from the world's largest continent

Euthenics \yoo–then–iks\: improving the human species through the improvement of...

Expose \ek'–spo–zay\: to make known;
reveal

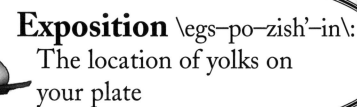

Exposition \egs–po–zish'–in\:
The location of yolks on
your plate

Ex Post Facto \eks' post fak'–to\:
after the fact

Extend \ik-stend'\: to stretch or draw
out to full length

Extension \egs-sten'-shin\:
When Humpty Dumpty
suffers from stress

Extensive \ik-sten'-siv\: comprehensive;
far-reaching

Extravehicular \ek'-stru-vee-hik'-yu-lur\: occurring outside an orbiting spacecraft

Extreme \eg-streem'\: A brook that Humpty Dumpty fishes in

Extremist \ik-stree'-mist\: a supporter of extreme doctrines or practices

Eyeball \I'-bol\: the globe of the eye
enclosed by the bony socket and eyelids

Eyeball \i'-bol\:
A social event for
optometrists

Eye Contact \I'-kontact\: visual
contact with another person's eyes

Eye \I\: the organ of sight

Eyebrows \i'-brous\: What I do when I go shopping

Eyebrows \I'-brous\: the bony ridge forming the upper part of the eye

Eyecup \I'-kup\: a small oval cup for applying liquid remedies

 Eyedropper \i'-drop-ur\: A clumsy opthomologist

Eyeful \I'-fool\: a thorough view

Fan \fan\: a device for producing a
current of air

 **Fanatic** \fan–at'–ik\:
Where you store fans for
the winter

Fanatical \fə-nat'-i-kul\: characterized
by an extreme zeal

Flea \flee\: a small, flattened, wingless, bloodsucking insect

Flea Market \flee'mar'-kit\: What the crooks did after stealing groceries

Fleck \flek\: a speck, a small bit

Forecastle \for'-kas'-ul\: living quarters for sailors

Foreclose \for–kloz'\: Why teens go to the mall

Foreclosure \for–kloz'–zhur\: to take away the right to redeem, especially a mortgage

Foundation \foun-day'-shun\: the
basis or groundwork

 **Founder** \foun'-der\:
What the searchers said when
they discovered the lost girl

Foundling \found'-ling\: an infant
found abandoned

Franc \frangk\: a medium of exchange, begun in France

Franchise \franch'iz\: What a person from France sees with

Francium \fran'see-um\: a radioactive element of the alkali metal group

Generalize \jen'-ur-u-liz\: to infer, especially a general principle

Generally \jen'-er-al-lee'\: The hero who led the south in the civil war

Generalship \jen'-ur-er-ship'\: the rank or duties of a general

Gingerly \jin'–jur–lee\: with great care
or caution

Ginger Snaps \jin'–jer snaps'\:
When the movie star on
Gilligan's Island goes nuts.

Gingham \ging'–um\: plain-weave
cotton fabric, usually striped or checked

Glade \glad\: an open space in a forest

Gladiator \glad'–e–ate–r\:
What the bear said about
the fish

Gladiolus \glad'–E–O–lus\: of the iris
family

68

Hairdo \har'-doo\: the style in which a person's hair is cut and arranged; coiffure

Hairdresser \har'-dres-ur\: Where Bugs Bunny keeps his underwear

Hairdressing \har'-dres-ing\: cutting or styling hair

Hatchery \hach'-u-ree\: a place for hatching eggs

Hatchet \hach'-it\: What you do with a chicken egg

Hatchling \hach'-ling\: a young bird, reptile, or fish recently emerged from an egg

Hermetic \hur-met'-ik\: made airtight
by fusion or sealing

Hermit \hur'-mit\:
What she catches the
baseball with

Hermitage \hur'-mi-tij\: retreat;
hideaway

Hernia \hur'–nee–u\: the protrusion of an organ or tissue, especially in the abdominal region

 **Heroes** \hee'rhos\: What a guy in a boat does

Heroic \hi–ro'–ik\: daring; noble

Hundred \hun'-drid\: a cardinal
number, ten times ten

Hundred Yard Dash
\hun'-drid yard' dash\:What
happens when a highway painting
machine gets stuck

Hundredth \hun'-dridth\: next after
the ninety-ninth

Infant \in-fant'\: anything in the first
stage of existence

 **Infantile** \in'-fen-tile\:
Ceramic floor covering
installed in the nursery

Infantry \in'-fun-tree\: soldiers or
military units that fight on foot

Infest \in-fest'\: to overrun to an
unwanted degree

Infidel \in'-fi-del\:
Where most Cuban fried
chicken winds up

Infield \in-feeld\: the area of a baseball
field bounded by the base lines

Informant \in-for'-munt\: a person
who informs or gives information

Information
\in-fer-ma'-shen\:
Usually how geese fly

Informative \in-for'-mu-tiv\: giving
information; instructive

Intestate \in–tes'–tat\: not having made a will

Intestine \in–tes'–tin\: Behind closed doors, taking an exam

Inti \in'–tee\: the basic monetary unit of Peru

Ipso Facto \ip'-so fak'-to\:by the fact
itself

Iran \i'-ran\:

A country between Iraq
and a hard place

Iranian \I-ray'-nee'-un\: pertaining to
Iran or its inhabitants

Kidnap \kid'-nap\: to carry off (a person)
by force, especially to extract ransom

Kidneys \kid'-nees\:
What a kid usually scrapes

Kidskin \kid'-skin\: leather made from
the skin of a young goat

Kindness \kind'–nis\: considerate or helpful; humane.

 **Kindred** \kin'–drid\:
The fear of relatives

Kine \kine\: Archaic:a plural of cow

Klamath \klam'-uth\: a member of an
American Indian people of Oregon

 **Kleenex** \klee'-neks\:
What you get when you wash
behind your ears

Kleptomania \klep'-tu-may'-mee-u\:
a compulsion to steal

Lactic \lak'–tik\: pertaining to, or obtained from milk

Lactose \lak'–tos\:
What you say when someone has no feet

Lacuna \lu–kyoo'–nu\: a gap or missing part, as in a manuscript

Landfall \land'–fol\: an approach to or sighting of land

Landfill \land'–fil\: What Mr. Donahue's flight instructor said

Landform \land'–form\: a specific geomorphic feature on the surface of the earth

Left \left\: having liberal views in politics

Left Bank \left' bangk'\:
What the robber did when his
bag was full of loot

Left Hand \left' hand \: on or to the left

Litigant \lit'–i–gunt\: a person engaged
in a lawsuit

Litigator \lit'–i–ga–ter'\:
The act of setting fire to an
amphibious reptile

Litigious \li–tij'–us\: inclined to dispute
or disagree; argumentative

Live \live\: to be alive

Liver \liv'−er\:
A thing that is not dead

Liverwort \liv'−ur−wurt\: any mosslike
bryophyte of the class Hepaticae

Love \luv\: a profoundly tender, passionate affection for another person

 **Lovable** \luv'–u–bul\: Affection for a male bovine

Lovebird \luv'–bird\: small parrots that exhibit affection for their mates

Mariner \mar'–u–nur\: a person who directs the navigation of a ship; sailor

Marionette \mar'–ee–ah–net\: What Frankie Avalon wanted to do in those beach movies

Marital \mar'–i–tl\: pertaining to the state of marriage

Mercerize \mur'–su–rize\: to treat
cotton fabric to increase strength

 **Merchandise**
\mur'–chen–diz\: What store
owners play yahtzee with

Merchandizing \mur–chundi'–zing\: to
buy and sell; trade

Meteroroid \mee'–tee–u–roid\: small
bodies of rock traveling through space

Meteorologist
\me'–te–yu–rol'–u–jist\:
A beefed up kidney doctor

Meter \mee'–tur\: the rhythmic element
in music

Meteorology \mee–tur–a–le–je\: a
  science that deals with the atmospheric...

 **Meter Man** \me'–ter man\:
A guy just 39.37 inches high

Methane \meth–ane\: a colorless, odor-
  less, flammable gas

Mignonette \min'–yu–net'\: small, fragrant, greenish white flowers

 **Migraine** \mi'–grane\:
What one wheat grower said
to the other

Migrant \mi'–grunt\: moves from place
to place to get work

Millionth \mil'-yunth\: coming last in a series of a million

Millipede \mil'-ee-peed\: Why there were stains on the White House carpet when the Bush's left

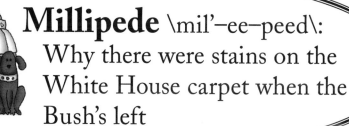

Millisecond \mil'-i-ske-und\: 1/1000 of a second

Minerva \mi–nur'–vu\: the Roman
goddess of wisdom and the arts

Minnesota \min'–i–so–dah\:
Describes a small carbonated
soft drink

Minestrone \min'–i–stro–hee\: a thick
vegetable soup, containing beans

Minuscule \min'-u-skyool\: very small

Minúte \mi-noot'\:  What Mama Gingrich calls her boy

Minuteman \min'-it-man\: American militia during the Revolutionary War

Mistrust \mis–trust'\: to regard with
mistrust, suspicion, or doubt; distrust

Misty \mis'–tee\:
How golfers create divots

Misunderstand \mis'–un–dur–stand'\:
to interpret incorrectly

Mobile \mo'-bul\: capable of being moved readily

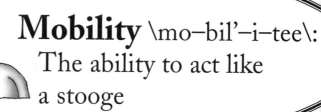 **Mobility** \mo-bil'-i-tee\: The ability to act like a stooge

Mobilize \mo'-bu-liz\: put into movement or action

Moray \mor'–a\: any tropical eel of the
family Muraenidae, lacking pectoral fins

Morbid \mor'–bid\:
A higher bid at an auction

Morbidity \mor'–bid'–i–tee\: a gruesome,
grisly quality

Munch \munch\: to chew steadily or
vigorously and often audibly

 **Munchkin** \munch'-kin\:
What cannibals do to
relatives

Mundane \mun-dayn\: common;
ordinary

Nature \na'-chur\: natural uncultivated scenery

Naughty \no'-tee\: Water or milk; for example

Nausea \no'-zhu\: sickness at the stomach; extreme disgust; loathing

Nettlesome \net'-l-sum\: Causing
irritation, vexation, or annoyance

 **Networks** \net'-wurks\:
What a successful
shrimper says

Neural \noor'-ul\: pertaining to a nerve
or the nervous system

Nickname \nik'–naym\: a name
substituted for the proper name

 **Nicotine** \nic'–u–teen\:
What usually happens to first
time shavers

Nictitate \nik'–ti–tat\: to wink

Nitpick \nit'–pik\: to criticize by focusing on minute details

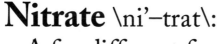 **Nitrate** \ni'–trat\:
A fee different from the charge during normal business hours

Nitre \ni'–tur\: nitrate, potassium nitrate; sodium nitrate

Nitrocellulose \ni'–tro–sel'–yu–los'\:
nitric esters of cellulose

Nitrogen \ni'–tru–jen\:
A soldier from Troy that
marches in the dark

Nitroglycerin \ni-tro–glis –ur–in\: a
highly explosive oily liquid

Nobility \no–bil'–i–tee\: persons
distinguished by rank or title

 **Noble** \no'–bul\:
A herd of only female
livestock

Nobleman \no'–bul–mun\: a man born
into distinguished birth, rank, or title

Nu \nyoo\: the 13th letter of the Greek
alphabet (N, n)

 **Nuance** \noo'-ans\:
The relatives you get when
your uncles re-marry

Nub \nub\: the point, gist, or heart of
something; a knob or protuberance

Orthodontics \or'–thu–don'–tiks\: the
prevention and correction of irregular teeth

 **Orthodox** \or'–tho–doks\:
A physician you seek when you
use too much weed killer

Orthgonal \or–thog'–u–hul\: involving
right angles or perpendiculars

Paradise \par'-u-dize\: a state of supreme happiness

Paradox \par'-u-doks\: Two physicians

Paraffin \par'-u-fin\: ...waxy, solid mixture of alkanes used in candles

Paralytic \par'-u-lit'-ik\: a person affected
with a loss or impairment of movement

 **Paralyze** \par'-u-liz\:
Two lies

Paramecium \par'-u-mee-she-um\:
a freshwater protozoan of the genus

Paraquat \par'–u–kwot\: a toxic herbicide

Parasites \par'–us–ites\: What you see from the top of the Eiffel Tower

Parasitic \par'–u–sit–ik\: living off the hospitality of others

Patristic \pu–tris'–tik\: pertaining to the fathers of the Christian church

 **Patrol** \pu–trol'\:
What a baby troll
calls his dad

Patrolman \pu–trol'–mun\: a police
officer who is assigned to patrol

Pepsin \pep'–sin\: an enzyme, produced in the stomach

 **Pepsodent** \pep–so'–dent\: When your car gets hit by a soft drink truck

Peptic \pep–tik\: a substance promoting digestion

Percolate \pur'–ku–lat'\: to brew
(coffee) in a percolator

Percolator \pur'–kue–la–ter\:
What the boss says when
he delays your bonus

Percussion \pur'–kush–un\: impact; blow

Pharmaceutical \far'–mu–soo–ti–kul\:
pertaining to...dispensing drugs

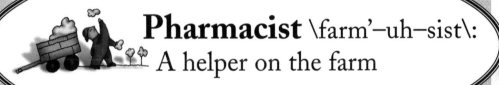

Pharmacist \farm'–uh–sist\:
A helper on the farm

Pharmacology \far'–mu–kol'–u–jee\:
dealing with the...effects of drugs

Pion \pi–on\: having positive, negative, or neutral electric charge and spin of zero

 **Pioneers** \pi–u–neers'\: What you get in a dessert food fight

Pious \pi–us\: sacred rather than secular

Polarization \po'-lur-I-zay'-shen\: a
sharp division

 **Polarize** \po'-lur-ize\:
What penguins see with

Polaroid \po'-lu-'roid \: the first brand of
instant camera

Pomade \po–made\: a scented ointment, especially for dressing the hair

Pomegranate
\pom'–gran–it\:
A petrified tropical tree

Pomeranian \pom'–a–ra–nee–un\: a breed of small dogs with long, straight hair

Pontificate \pon–tif'–i–kit\: to speak in
a pompous or dogmatic manner

Pontoon \pon–toon'\:
An animated feature starring
a minor chess piece

Pony \po–nee\: a small horse

118

Popcorn \pop'–korn\: corn whose kernels burst open and puff out

Popcorn Ball

\pop'–korn bol'\:
What corn-ball's call
their dad

Pope \pope\: the bishop of Rome as head of the Roman Catholic Church

Primary \pri'–mer'–ee\: first in rank or importance; chief

 **Primate** \pri'–mat\: Removing your spouse from in front of the TV

Prime \prim\: of the first importance

Propose \pru-poz\: to offer for
consideration, acceptance, or action

Proposition \prop–u–zish'–en\:
What you should notice when
walking near an airplane

Propound \pru-pound \: offer for
consideration, acceptance, or adoption

121

Pyjama \pu-ja'-mu\: pajama

Pylon \pi'-lon\:
What the football players do
on a tackle play

Pyorrhea \pi'-u-'-lee-'a\: a discharge
of pus

Quibble \kwib'–el\: a petty or carping criticism

 **Quiche** \keesh'\: What the Gabors pucker up for

Quick \kwik\: occurring with promptness or rapidity

Radiant \ra'-dee-unt\: emitting rays of
light; shining; bright

Radiate \rad'-ee-at\:
Why the roach died

Radiation \ray'-dee-A-shun\: the
process in which energy is emitted

Realtor \ree'–ul–tur\: a person in the real-estate business

Realty \ree'–ul–tee\: Brewed from a bag, not instant

Ream \reem\: a standard quantity of paper

Recapture \ri-cap-ture\: to capture again; retake

 **Recede** \ri-seed'\:
When you're washed out and
have to plant again

Receipt \ri-seet\: a written acknowledgment of having received money or goods

Relic \rel'–lik\: a surviving trace of
something

Relief \ri–leef'\:
What trees do in the spring

Relieve \ri–leev\: to ease or alleviate

127

Requiem \rek'–wee–um\: any musical
service or hymn for the repose of the dead

Require \ree-kwir'\:
What the music director did
when all the singers quit

Required \ri-kwird\: necessary or
indispensable

Rubberize \rub'-u-rize\: to coat or impregnate with rubber

Rubberneck \rub'-er-nek\: What you do to relax your wife

Rubber Stamp \rub'-u-stamp'\: giving approval automatically or routinely

129

Rut \rut\: a fixed mode of procedure or course of life

Rutabaga \roo'-tuh-ba'-guh\: A panhandler with no manners

Ruth \rooth\: a book of the Bible in the Old Testament

Sandhog \sand'-hog\: a person who
works in... digging underwater tunnels

San Diego \san-dee'-eg-o\:
When you drop your toaster
waffle on the beach

Sandlot \sand'-lot\: a vacant lot used by
youngsters for games or sports

Sateen \sa-teen'\: a cotton fabric constructed in satin weave

Satellite \sat'-l-lite\: What you put on your horse to go riding at night

Satiate \say-shee-ate\: satisfy fully, as in appetite or desire

Seafarer \see'-far'-ur\: a traveler on the sea; sailor

Seafoam \see'-fom\: How to tell if a dog is rabid

Seafood \see'-food\: any fish or shellfish from the sea used for food

Seamanship \see'–mun–ship\: skill
pertaining to the navigation of a ship

 **Seamstress** \seem'–stris\:
Describes 250 pounds in a
size six

Seamy \see–mee\: sordid; low;
disagreeable

134

Self-interest \self'–in'–trist\: personal interest or advantage

 **Selfish** \sel'–fish\: What the owner of a seafood store does

Self-knowledge \self'–nol'–ij\: understanding of oneself and one's character

135

Senescent \si–nes'–unt\: growing old; aging

Senile \see'–nile\:
What you say when you see
the largest river in Egypt

Senility \si–nil'–i–tee\: the weakness or mental infirmity of old age

Slipcover \slip'–kuv–ur\: a cover made so
as to be easily removable

Slipknot \slip'–not\:

An admonition not to fall on
the ice; as quoted in the King
James Version

Slip-on \slip'–on\: made to be put on
easily and quickly

Sorely \sor'lee\: extremely; very

Sorghum \sor'–gum\:
A periodontal disease

Sorority \su-for'-i-tee\: a society of
women or girls, especially in a college

Spirea \spy–ree'–a\: any shrub of the genus Spiraea, of the rose family

Spirit \speer'–it\:
What Captain Ahab wanted
to do to Moby Dick

Spirited \spir–i–tid\: having or showing
mettle, courage, vigor, or animation

Stage \staj\: a phase, degree, or step in a process

Stagecoach \staj'-koch\: What you call a play's director

Stagecraft \staj'-kraft\: the art of writing, adapting, or staging plays

Stale \stal\: musty; stagnant

Stalemate \stal'–mat\:
How an Australian describes
old bread

Stalinism \sta'-lu-niz'-um\: associated
with Stalin, characterized by...suppression

Steeplejack \stee'–pul–jak'\: a person who climbs steeples to build or repair them

 **Steering** \steer'–ing\: What the bull gave the cow when they were married

Steerage \stir'–ij\: management; direction

Subdivision \sub'–di–vizh'–un\: a
division of a larger division

Subdued \sub–dood'\:
Like, a guy who, like, works
on one of those, like sub-
marines, man

Subentry \sub'–en'–tre\: an entry (as in an
account) made under a more general entry

143

Suction \suk'–shun\: to draw out or remove by aspiration

 **Sudafed** \sood'–a–fed\:
Bringing litigation against a
government official

Sudden \sud'–n\: done quickly, without warning, or unexpectedly

Sumerian \soo–mir'–ee–un\: pertaining to Sumer, its people, or their language

Summarize \sum'–ur–ize\: Optical nerves that have adjusted to the heat and light

Summary \sum'–u–ree\: brief and comprehensive; concise

Sybaritic \sib'-u-rit'-ik\: pertaining to Sybaris or its residents

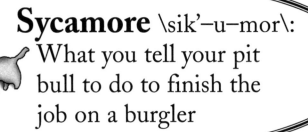

Sycamore \sik'-u-mor\: What you tell your pit bull to do to finish the job on a burglar

Sycophancy \sik'-u-fun-see\: self-seeking or servile flattery

Tartar \ta'–tur\: the deposit from wines

 **Tater Tots** \ta'–tur tots\: The children of couch potatoes

Tatter \tat'–ur\: a separate torn piece; shred

Toilet \toi'-lit\: a bathroom or washroom

 **Toiletries** \toi'-li-trees\: Describes a forest in the bathroom

Toilette \twa-let\: Archaic: a dressing table

Tolerable \tol'-ur-u-bul\: endurable

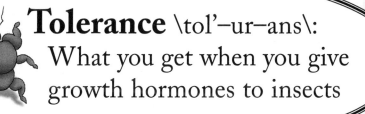

Tolerance \tol'-ur-ans\:
What you get when you give
growth hormones to insects

Tolerant \tol'-ur-unt\: forbearing

Toughen \tuf'-en\: to make strong and durable

Toupee \too'-pa\: Why you go to the checkout

Tour \toor\: traveling around from place to place

Tweeter \twee'–tur\: a small loudspeaker
for the reproduction of high-frequency sounds

 **Tweeze** \tweez\:
What Elmer Fudd finds
in the forest

Tweezers \twee'–zurz\: small pincers or
nippers for plucking out hairs

Uzbek \ooz'–bek'\: a member of a Turkic
people of Uzbekistan

Vacancy \va'–kun–see\:
A sea with no contents

Vacant \va–kunt\: having no contents;
empty; void

Vitals \vit'–lz\: the essential parts of something

Vitamin \vi'–tu–min\:  What you do when friends drop by for a visit

Vitiate \vish'–ee–ate\: to impair or weaken the effectiveness of

Warder\wor'–dur\: a doorkeeper

Wardrobe \wor'–drob\:
What Beaver Cleaver's dad
wore around the house

Wardroom \word–room \: living and
dining quarters...for all commissioned officers

Weird \wird\: strange; unusual; peculiar

Weirdo \wir'-do\:
What you make weird
bread with

Welch \welch\: natives of Wales

155

Windmill \wind'–mil\: machines for grinding, driven by the force of the wind

Window \win'–do\: The act of winning money

Windowpane \win'–do–payn\: a plate of glass for filling a window sash

Withdraw \with-dro'\: 1. to draw back, away, or aside

Withdrawal \with-drah'-ul\: How people in Texas talk

Withdrawn \with-dron\: shy and introverted; retiring

About the Author

Jim Marble's hard-to-remember real name is Marable, the grandson of New Mexico homesteaders, and has spent the last decade in love with the people of Tulsa, Oklahoma while dreaming of the mountains back home.

Jim Marbles has been in broadcasting since the Earth cooled, and men were mindless, barbaric animals in paisley and bell-bottoms. Though a morning show host by nature, he has also been a TV weatherman, gameshow host and co-host of Southwest Showcase of Homes. Along the way, he has picked up such commendations as morning man at "Billboard Magazine Country Station of the Year" for two years in a row, "Best of Albuquerque", "Best of Tulsa" and was one of three nominees for Oklahoma Broadcaster of the Year 1994.

He walked away from the bottomless pit of despair and stress that is secular radio to return to his first love, Christian broadcasting, in mid-1994. He was fortunate to sign on with a meteorically-rising, home owned station, KXOJ, that was named by *Religion and the Media Quarterly* as the nation's Contemporary Christian Station of the Year in 1996.

His is continually peeved by people coming up to his wife of 18 years and saying "you poor thing—how do you put up with him?" His wife, Georgi, is a retirement center administrator, and both are cultivating premature gray hair due to their teenage son Jonathan.

Jim Marbles has no spare time, but if he had, would enjoy archeology, channel surfing and construction projects. He currently is an accomplished artist whose works are displayed almost entirely on his mother's refrigerator.

Additional copies of this book
are available from your local bookstore.

Trade Life Books, Inc.
Tulsa, Oklahoma